Greta Juli

Tarned As The Sun

Poetry & Prose

AF236192

1

Impressum

Bibliografische Information der Deutschen
Nationalbibliothek:
Die Deutsche Nationalbibliothek verzeichnet diese
Publikation in der Deutschen
Nationalbibliografie; detaillierte bibliografische Daten
sind im Internet über www.dnb.de abrufbar.

© Greta Juli
 Herstellung und Verlag:
 BoD - Books on Demand, Norderstedt
 ISBN: 9783752625813

Über die Autorin:

Greta Juli ist eine junge Autorin aus Essen. Ihr erstes Buch schrieb sie bereits mit zwölf Jahren. Darauf folgten viele weitere Romane, die sich hauptsächlich mit den Themen Coming of Age, Schicksalsschläge sowie Freundschaft und Liebe beschäftigen.
Tarned As The Sun ist ihr erstes Poetry-Buch, welches sie mit siebzehn Jahren ebenfalls zum ersten Mal auf Englisch verfasste.
Gerade schreibt sie an ihrem zweiten Werk im gleichen Stil von *Tarned As The Sun*.

Greta Juli is a young author from Essen Germany. She wrote her first book at the age of twelve. This was followed by many other novels which mainly deal with the topics of coming of age, strokes of fate as well as friendship and love.
Tarned As The Sun is her first poetry book which she also wrote in English for the first time when she was seventeen.
She is currently working on her second work in the same style like *Tarned As The Sun*.

Tarned As The Sun

Here speaks the soul of a broken heart
trying to find her voice back
after an enigmatic storm came (tarned as the beautiful
sun)
took away her words, her mind
and left nothing behind than
silence

- So here I come back

Stronger

when you are at the edge
on the ground
on the ugly truth
on the bitter place of your own
time
after
time
you become stronger and braver
and
more you
than ever before,
trust me,
braver
and
stronger
and
you, you, you.

- time is a healer

You said

First you said you need time
You said you´re not sure about everything
You said okay, let´s talk
You said you just see me as a friend anymore
You said please, don´t cry
You said you´ll find the right one, one day
You said we still can be friends
Me, desperate and broken, said „okay"
I wrote to you, many times
And than
in spite of all your words
and promises
you never said anything to me
again

- It´s you´re cowardice which hurts me most

Pain

Before I met you
I never knew how love feels like,
before I met you,
I never knew how happiness is like,
before I met you,
I never knew
that the hardest pain is the one
which comes from your heart,
a broken, destroyed heart,
sets up his ashes
through your whole body
like a fire in a forest
leaving nothing behind than
the
smell
of
hurting

Mirror

After you left I became a ghost, my mom puts me to
many people, trying to make me whole again.
I remember this woman with those shiny eyes and the
calm smile. What she said to me, after she made some
energy exercises, which should help me through the
days.
She wrote some things on a small paper, gave it to me
and said that I should read them a few times a day.
One sentence I didn´t understand that time:

I am the most important person in my life.

All I thought was no: The most important person in my
life left me a month ago.
But today I understand what she meant with that.
You are your own, you are the one you should love
through your whole life.
You should be your own best friend, your helper, your
healer,
the one,
you should care the most,
without being selfish.

Because the souls come and go through your entire life.

But your own soul will stay forever with you.

So come on and start loving you.

Waiting

Tell me,
what do you need now?
Tell me,
do you need somebody who embraces you?
Tell me,
what do you need, darling, when you´re sitting
each day alone, in the shadow,
like waiting for the sun.
Tell me,
do you need somebody who gives you light?
Tell me
what you need.
Because maybe
I need the same
and we can
collect our hopeful feelings,
becoming *one* little mess.

- *Sometimes we just need to talk*

Miracle

Sometimes you know only a miracle can save your day
Sometimes you know a miracle will not happen
Sometimes you know everything is hopeless
Sometimes you don´t know that your miracle
was already there
But you just not recognized it

*- So, how do you think about me, when you look back to
the old days?*

Like the biggest fault

Sometimes, when I can´t sleep because my thoughts are
running and running, whirling around you, I ask myself
if you ever have this feeling of loneliness, if you´re
laying in your bed, next to you: emptiness, a place
where I was before you let me go.
And I wonder if you ever feel alone, regretting that you
left me, looking at it like the biggest fault you ever
made in your whole life.

Lonely

When you´re surrounded by hundred of people, all of
them talk and some with you,
when the sun shines so strongly and the roads are full of
happy people, smiling faces,
when you´re sitting in your room, talking with your
mom, a few minutes later with your sister
and then with you´re cat, about your day, about your
life, about everything,
when the whole world grins at you
but
you
still feel like
the loneliest person in the universe

- For me, that describes the *feeling of loneliness*

Flowers

You can not see them
because they are growing underneeth your skin,
you can not reach them
because they are too far away from your mind,
but you should know,
deep inside you
there are flowers
colourful and beautiful
spreading all over your aches and sores and scars,
healing you
time
after
time

Your words, still there

„Do you know how georgeous you are?"

„Really?"

„Yes. So georgeous… How did I earn that?"

So georgeous,
your words, still in my head,
now,
starring at my chocolate bar,
asking myself if it was true
what you said,
deciding *no*,
putting the candy back into the shelf
and myself, my old, confident mind, too,
right beside

- Heartbreak should never break your body, so please,
eat the chocolate

Mom

I want to apologize
for every word too hard
for every scream too loud
for every ache too strong
just because young humans
sometimes don´t know
how to excist

so thank you for always giving me a warm place
in an often too cold and windy world

- I love you

Fix me

Can someone please come
and fix me?
Because I feel small
and fragile.
Tell me,
is there any chance
to
fix me?
When not,
there is the possibility
that I will fly away with the wind,
becoming
dust.

Control

It´s easy for me to loose control.
Sometimes I feel like a wreck, and I really mean like a
wreck, for example when something does not work like
I planned it. When I wanted the small popcorn size but
my Mom decided spontaniously to share a large portion
with me. When I was looking forward to my favourite
series, the whole day, but my family would rather see
something different.
When I sleep two minutes longer after my alarm clock
rings, when I don´t make notices of all the things which
I have to do, when some things aren´t decided on my
own, when other people, the chance, the destiny or
something like that, decides for me.
The „what could have been" sometimes takes a too big
role in my life, because I´m always on the run to plan
the things, the days, the weeks, everything, than just
living my life without fear, being brave and valiant.
I wait for the day when I begin to let go, all the things
and determine that sometimes it is okay
only to breath.
Breathing without any plans.

Back

Sometimes there are days when I want you back
when I forget what you made with my heart
when I forget how you treated me
what type of boy you developed in our whole lovestory.
But when I remember
I take a deep breath and wonder
why I ever
wanted you
back.

How?

How can you
treat me like I am
nothing
after you once said I am your
everything?

Our last night

I often think about our
last night
when I layed in your arms
safe and sound
felt our broken relation
but was so happy not being alone
was so afraid of being alone
so I whispered
as soft as I could
„I am so happy that I got you"
and everything you said was
nothing
apart from a little
embarrassed laugh

- That was the moment I knew it would be over soon

If I die

If I ever die, I want them to howl and drown in their tears, so I know it wasn´t for nothing.

Thank you

Last night
you were by my side
and I felt
prettier
than
ever

Words

your words helped me through this hell

- words are saviors

All I can do

every
new
day
is
a
blank
room
i
want
to
fill
with
colors
and
clearness,
but
all
i
can
do
is
fixing
my
thoughts
for
keeping
me
away
from
this

hurricane
inside
my
veins

- again, again

Thin

sometimes

i

want

to

fade

to

thin

p
a
p
e
r

and than drifting
away with the wind

Never a waste of time

all the flowers in you make me grow like i was never a
waste of time

- and you do not even need water to keep me alive

About growing

„You grow to become beautiful",
they say or think.
But no,
you grow to find yourself
with being your beautiful
truth.

- That's what growing is about

Sisters

Sisters
might
be
the
answer
of
the
question:
Is there anything that is stronger than   ?

You

you. make. me. bloom.

To my old me

It get´s better. When somebody steals your universe and
the people say that time will make it easier,
it´s okay when you don´t believe it. When you think that
your life is over. It´s okay to cry a whole river, to feel
like a broken mess, like a fool, worthless.
There will be a day when you stop crying at the
evening, when you look at him and hears his voice and
the pain is not as strong as usual.
Keep your head above the water. Love is a mystery. But
you will learn to live with feeling half.

You will survive.

Love,
your present you

See you clearer now

Once I thought the people are all the same, only I am
different. Once I thought nobody ever feels so lost and
lonely like I did. I thought there is a difference between
open minded and shy.
Between loud and quiet. Friendly and rude. Happy and
sad. You and me.
Nothing in between.
But the years opened my eyes, I went out of my safety
comfort zone, met knew people and now I know
that there are universes and galaxys that make people
different from each other.
That we are all so different but with some so close
*and that makes it easier when I sometimes feel lost in
this world.*

One year

Crazy how much
your life can change
in just one year,
crazy how much your feelings can change
in just one year,
crazy how many friends you can win and loose,
in just one year,
crazy how you can turn from a damsel
into a princess
in just
one year,
and crazy how fast you can
fall back to where you came from
in just one year.

Until

I never thought I could be brave until I met you.

July

holding
our
polaroid
in
my
hands
and
remember
the
old
time
when
we
both
didn't
knew
that
those
moments
will
become
the
ones
we
wish
back

- i'm sorry for what i've said, my old friend

Touch me

The moment when you touch me:
Like
butterflies
are growing
underneath
my
skin.

Only a fraction

i like the idea
that the universe
is only a fraction
of what we see
and actually
there is something
much bigger than this
and nothing is so important
as we always suspect

Start now

b e a u t y

                begins

when you learn to eliminate the

          b e a s t

inside your veins

Now, the romantic part of me speaks

sometimes
when
i
look into your deep green eyes,
i wish
that we marry and make sweet childs,
live in a big house near to the park,
with daddy and mummy and little juniors,
getting old, getting so old, day by day,
our babies, see, they´re growin´ so tall,
letting the days drifting by, greeting our
lost friends at the supermarket,
becoming grey and white.
but together.
dying at the park bench in front of our house.
together.
forever.

Breaking

Breaking is similar to falling
only that when you fall
you first fly
before you break

Why we still believe in beauty

f l o w e r s

flowers,

the whole

big

world

needs

f l o w e r s

(not because they make everything better, with covering
up, no, because they are the reason why we still believe
in beautiful things, through everything)

S m o k e

I often notice that the smell of smoke is still something
beautiful for me.
Like the smell of cinnamon or mint for some others
smoke will forever be
the thing which
makes me feel warm,

because it reminds me of you,
standing there
with your cigarette.
So cool,
you were.
Damn,
so fucking cool.

Evil spirits

All the evil spirits think they make me small
but all the evil spirits are the ones which give me the
inspiration
for the art I create when I pave my wounds

- Words are my colour and this paper is the canvas for
all the unvoiced

Poetry

and
after
seventeen
years
of
living,
poetry
seems
to
be
the
thing
which
became
my
voice
for
all
the
silence
inside
my
soul

Don´t want to be nice anymore

I hope you´re somewhere outside
hope you cry sometimes because now I´m gone,
hope your lonely and lost like I was,
hope you find the right one but always remember
that you let go
the best you ever had.

Grow

in the absence of selfhate, i began to grow

Blank Papers

Sometimes I feel like
we´re all blank papers
at the begin of our birth
and love give´s us the
face and colours which
transform us into art

- You have created me with the brushes of your affection

Feelings

It is not always easy for me to talk about feelings,
because most of the time my feelings are mixed and
sometimes I can not describe them. But when I write, I
see my feelings clear, like they live inside my pen and
come to life with every word I use.
Maybe they feel more comfortable on papers.

Again, and again

When somebody
tells you
he has
some problems
and you ask what,
and he says
it´s not important,
than there´s probably
nothing more in his mind
than telling you
what´s going on.

- So maybe you have to ask again, and again, until he speaks

Moon

A look to the moon
reminds me
reminds me of you
when you said
that sometimes
you look to the moon
and tells him all your secrets
like he is your friend
and this thought
reminds me
of hating the moon
because he is so close to you
while I´m trying to
get as far away as I can
from you

Happy

When I am happy my body is filled with a bright light,
spreading through my blood and then I can´t stop
feeling so lightly,
like the sun lives inside my bones

Sunday evening

hear your song
in those trains
hear your voice
singing my name
oh, what a beautiful,
beautiful evening,
want to hold on,
want to hold this world,
in my hands
walking to your house,
ringing, you,
opening with this surprising smile,
i smile too,
and say i love you,
let´s walk to sweden and built a
house and stay there forever together
and forget this old world,
and you laugh and take my hand
and squeeze it for two times and
i do it too,
so you say
what do you want at my door at 2 pm?
oh, baby, i only want to see you
at this beautiful,
beautiful
sunday
evening

No!

too
soon
too
high
too
late
too
ugly
too
pretty
too
raw
too
straight
too
thin
too
fat
too
cool
too
fake
too
afraid
too
alone
too
much
too

good
for
you

- *no*

After Everything

After all this time, after living the last half year, I
learned that life can stop, fall apart, break, not exist
anymore and the person you once was, can never be
fixed. But after the storm, after surviving, it will be
better, you become another you, but you see the world
in a different way, you see you in a different way,
because now you know your torches, your aches, your
pain and tears at the best, so that makes you see how
strong and brave your bruises made you.
Life goes on.
Believe me.
Life. Will. Go. On.

Jealous

Sometimes I am jealous.
Jealous of my old me,
of the brave, lively and
powerful girl who went
to parties, who stayed
the whole night awake,
who kissed,
who lived, who loved,
so free.
But then I remember
that this girl is not another
person.
This girl I wish back is
still me,
still here.
I am
still here,
I am
still the same.
The same as yesterday,
the same as now
the same as tomorrow.
So here we are.

...

waiting
for
the
scream
while
sticking
in
my
silence

...

Better

Before I met you,
I´d never know that there is
somethingmoreimportantthanwriting,
now,
you taught me something better.

Prettier

„ You are prettier without this make up shit "

- But **I** like it

First Kiss

It was a thursday in February, one day after Valentines
Day.
You starred at me and than I starred at you.
And than we kissed.
Magic.
And I stayed the same girl
like before,
but maybe I became more selfconfident, in relation to
myself,
because I thought:
Do you see? Sometimes all this selfhate is so absurd,
because there are lips on your lips,
lips which makes you feel
worth.
Loved.

Kill those words

„this girl is fat"

„this girl is ugly"

„this girl should kill herself"

„this boy is ridiculous"

„this boy is an indulgence for my eyes"

„this boy should kill himself"

- Just as we create words, we have to kill some of them

nobody in this world should kill himself, nobody,
nobody, nobody

Now

Always thinking about my future,
about what will happen and what
will never ever become my life
instead of thinking what I got,
what happened in the past and what
and who I am,
now.

The reason

your face is the reason
why I can finally breathe again

Wings

I grew up with those wings,
they brought me to different places,
to so many faces,
and sometimes they broke and I
layed down, on the ground,
only me and my broken strings.
But at least
I am here and I fly,
even you took my wings
and crumpled them to little pieces.
Do you see *me*?
Flying above your head
seeing you as just
a little tiny dot.

Still on his way

There is nothing which is important, my dear,
there is nothing to worry about,
no reason to waist tears for that boy,
no reason you should love him anymore,
because the fact
that he left you, darling,
this beautiful wonder,
is enough, that he can not be the right one,
that he was just a thankful experience,
something,
which enriched your life, something,
which will make you grow in a half year,
when the pain is almost over,
and I know,
he is away
but you are still here and you should know that,
little girl,
it is not the end of the world and it was the best thing
that could happened to you,
that he left you,
because, believe me,
the prince is on his way time after time
you will see that I was right.

Pretty

Pretty people
are everywhere
but pretty hearts,
I can not see them,
can you show
me one,
anywhere,
here in that place?

Papa

It was always you
who reminded me
I have a voice.

Always you
who helped me
to find my words
when I had feared to
loose them.

It will always be you
who will show me
that yes,
I can be the one
the world has
waited for.

The opposite of loneliness

I told you:
The opposite of loneliness is love.
And with you I can never be lonely.

You told me:
I will never leave you.
I will never make you feel lonely.

And now,
I´m sitting here,
swimming in my loneliness,
a river
of all your lies.

Like Prison

Every breath,
every step,
every thought,
so controlled,
that sometimes
this girl feels
like she´s living
in a prison,
with closed
doors and no
sun light,
only the darkness,
and
day by day,
she tries to
break out,
but there are
ties on her bones,
saying her
that in a prison
it´s safer,
that the real
dangerous world
outside
can not touch her

- But she wants nothing more than to touch the real

Opposites

You was the one everybody noticed,
loud and always present,
I was the one the most forget I exist,
silent and shy.

It were the opposites which
brought us together.

And it were the opposites
that tore us apart.

Rush

our love was a rush.
and you was the drug I
was addicted to.
but you,
yes, you had
your own drugs,
and it was not me,
it was
something in a
little plastic bag,
something
more important
than my
existence
ever was
for you.

Future me

When they ask me
about my future
I tell them a lie,
because
I don´t know
which person I will be
because I don´t know what time
will create
what life will make with me,
so why
do they all want to know
who I become,
instead of asking
who
I
am
?!

What makes me happy?

I needed a lot of time to answer this question.
The last months were like walking through all four
seasons and now I feel wiser,
I know me better than ever before.

And I know
that a normal day, one, without chaos and tears,
when I´m not alone,
with a cup of tea and my favourite crackers
and chocolate,
sitting in front of the TV, just relaxing with my mom
and breathing,
that
makes me happy and it´s okay.

Wearing The Love

I like the smile you wear on saturday,
I hate the fury you wear on sunday
and I love the love you wear
whenever
you´re with me.

Baby

I miss you baby,
I miss you so much
Baby?
Is everything okay?

There was a time I was sometimes annoyed of those
„Baby"-things,
but now,
there are days I wish nothing more than hundred of
those messages from you,
asking me If I still live,
only because I´m not online
for five minutes.

Out Of Town

You´re somewhere outside,
out of town,
out of our house,
far away from home
and first I was happy
for the silence you left
since you´re not here anymore
but now
I miss the chaos, the screaming,
the troubles and the love
you created
when you were here.

Hope you are brave and do not feel alone so far away
from us, living in this new strange world.

Everything

In that moment some things
may seem to be too tough
to come along with,
too tricky and too destroyed,
but listen to me,
let me tell you something.
I am sure that the things
will make their way,
that you will go your way
and at the end you´ll look back
and think,
how afraid how insecure you were
about that unknown future
and than you will smile,
into your soul
and see,
that everything
somehow
went good

Death

I'm afraid of death. I am afraid to give up everything
called my life, everything I created, I lived for, I loved
for, I was for. Letting go was never one of my strength,
but the death seems to me like a big challenge,
something I can not handle. Getting out of light and
shadow, leaving the world without knowing what comes
next, the unplanned, the surprise, this is also one of the
things I'm afraid of.
But now,
I remember myself that
I live,
because sometimes,
when I think too much about what will happen
I get lost in my thoughts.
but now,
I am here and I live.
and the death is something which will surely happen
and maybe that's one of the strangest things of it. That
you can't control, influence it.
The day will come and I hope I will be a person which
isn't sad about leaving this place,
rather someone who is excited of what

No robot

You could had
make it better
You should had
make it better
You must
make it better

I made it like I breathe
- automatically, because I am no robot

What I am

I am my fears
I am my tears
I am my strength
I am my ghost
I am my story
I am my past
I am my now
I am my bruises
I am my fury
I am my love
I am my thoughts
I am my fight
I am my mom
I am my dad
I am my sister
I am my friends
I am my ex's
I am my future
I am my hope
I am my dark
I am my light
I am you
I always be me

And I am
a
l o t

Help me

It is okay, the ghosts inside me, the mountains I have to
climb,
the strings in me, the wounds under my skin,
I can endure a lot,
I accepted to endure a lot,
but now is the moment
I can´t.
all my cards, building a house, are destroyed,
again.
I
just can´t keep the things together
anymore.
I am done,
and I don´t want to stand up
and I ask myself
why me,
why always always me,
why not the boy on the other side of the street?
Why the hell always me?
And I breathe and I cry and I don´t want to stop my
tears
because this time,
I let go,
so,
help me,
whoever.

Little things

hurt the most, because you´re trying to suppress the pain
and with that it gets harder to get free of it

Pity

The moment you get pity with you is the moment you
start to build love for yourself

Embrace

embrace me
embrace me
because I need
someone
who tells my body
that
he's
perfect

Something

I try´d to be you
I try´d to be your shadow
try´d to be your mirror
to be your contour
be your skin
your soul
something
something to
something to believe
something to believe in

- But then I started to believe in myself

I don´t need you anymore

There was a time
I could not fall in love again without you
I could not fall asleep without you
I could not live my days without you
But now the time passed by
and I´m able and proud to say
that
I can fall in love
I can fall asleep
I can live and I can breathe
without you
and I don´t need you anymore
to give my life a sense

I don´t need you anymore

Blackbirds singing

Hey,
old friend,
I just want to say
that sometimes I
think I´m too lonley
too boring
too everything
because I´m not the one with million
friends,
but then I remember, that you are
on my side since we are little,
and than I think
that one friend can be more than
hundred,
because you´re worth, you´re wonderful
when someone
calls you
your best friend,
one in a million,
and it´s you,
who is destined
to be the best friend
it´s you.

Heartbreak can be some kind of magic

You hold my hand when he broke my heart.
Now I´m the one who drys your tears
because you decided to broke yours too
and that´s some kind of crazy and nice,
in a weird way.

Because this heartbreaking brought us more together
than everything before.

Love

I thought I can only be full with love when I´m in love
with somebody.
But the last months taught me something better.

You can be in love in every way,
With loving your lover,
with loving your life,
with loving yourself,
with loving the people around you,
with loving your future love,
with loving your first love,
with loving the love,
so
don´t think love only can be part of you
when you are in a relationship.

When you once loved,
love will never leave you.

A Part of Everything

Sometimes I´m just so thankful.
For breathing, for living, for existing.
For just being there in the moment,
for being a part of this world.
A part of everything.

Fade

I am a flower and sometimes I fade.
But I can survive
because I am a flower and flowers
can live again
after they fade.

So can you see my new georgeous colours?

Daughter

I am your daughter,
the one who´s there
because of you,
so I hope everyday
I can make you proud
that the egg cell
became
me

Believe me

Believe me,
you have a talent,
even it seems to be boring
and usual and so not special,
you have a talent,
you are brilliant
you are magical,
you can change everything.

I need no fairytale anymore

I´m not anymore that girl who wants a fairytale-
lovestory,
the prince with the white horse and the castle and the
diamonds.
Because when you want those things,
you should know that you can fall deep,
very deep,
from castle to cottage,
from diamonds to stones,
and then you look around and ask yourself why you
ever could
trust that fairytale,
because you realize
that fairytales got the tricky thing that they are not
r e a l.

The Sun Will Come Up

You feel lonely and sad
and you fear that feeling will never go,
that there will always be rain
and you will always be broken.
But the sun will come up again,
you will feel better,
you will feel happy and you will look
at your life
and you will smile,
because it is yours,
yours.
So don´t give up.

Seeing you

Seeing you hurted me like walking through a forest fire.
But now.
I see you and I see you and I remember that you exist,
and then I just keep living my life.
What else should I do?

I see you and I survive.

WE ARE BEAUTIFUL

we are just beautiful creatures, so don´t look at us like
we are nothing
because we are BEAUTIFUL and we are young and
dumb and we are
so insecure and selfconfident and loud and quiet but we
are
BEAUTIFUL
because we are not afraid
of being who we are even if we are someone else
so don´t tell me we are not
BEAUTIFUL

What will happen,
eighteen?

You are sixteen and you fall in love and your life
becomes love from one day to another.
They say, it´s the edge of seventeen, the time when you
cry and scream and love and loose
and die and survive.
And they say
you begin to become adult,
you know who you are,
when you are eighteen.

Now I´m sitting here,
asking myself if the people are right,
if I will know who I am,
because the sixteen´ and seventeen´ clichees
just fit perfectly to my life.

Edit: The eighteen clichee is a damn lie to my life

Shy

„Your presentation was good, but you are just too shy,
as you probably know"

I hate it when people are calling me shy.
Because it always seems to be something wrong,
when you´re just not so selfconfident like others,
as if it deviate from the norm, just not right,
not being how you normally should.

But there is no basis that determines how one has to be.
There is no ideal.

So don´t call me shy.

Shy people are always seen as wrong.

And I am not wrong.

I am enough,
so call me quiet,
call me sensitive,
the opposite of loud,
calm,
but not

shy.

Nobody is shy.

Wires

I want to see the whole world clear, always. Want to
absorb everything, think correctly, work, being free.
But so often
there are invisible wires that influence me, wrap me and
then it´s like I´m underwater,
feeling nothing.
So give me your hand and bring me back to air.

Watching you fall

You had that dreams you told me about and I knew how
important there were for you. And now,
you are without me and everybody sees that you got
problems, and I won´t but I catch myself
by feeling pity with you.
Because I remember us,
you in my arms, with our dreams and our tiredness and
frivolity.
I knew you would go lost without me,
but now I feel guilty for the one you become without
me,
even through
you were the one who left me.

Maybe that´s your way and it should be like this.

Maybe everything should be as it is.

But… you were better with me.

Cry

Sometimes I am happy,
but there is something which knocks me down,
so I can´t be me anymore,
I just cry, because there is something which makes
me so sad,
inspite I am happy.
This is crazy and I hate this mixture of feelings.

Take care

You should take care,
you should take care of yourself,
when giving your everything,
giving your love:
the most fragile thing you carry with you.

Smile to the one you like
kiss the one you love
live for them who need you
but never forget
that people can hurt.

Strange

It´s strange how we grew old,
how we changed,
what we lived and how we lived,
time passed by
and now,
we are here,
so isn´t it strange
that at the end
we are still the same?

Even if nothing ever stays same.

We.

We stay.

Just okay

So often I feel okay,
there is no big problem,
everything okay.
But then there is the feeling
that something is missing
which makes me feel happy.
Sometimes
I just want to feel
completely.

But thats so difficult
after you left.

Edge

„I think I´m on the edge"

„Than... go back to the start"

Hearts

Why do our hearts
always choose the ones
who hurt us most?

Holding you

I will tell you a secret.
Sometimes I see a strange boy and I imagine how I
would hold him,
embracing him with the feeling of being loved.

Sometimes I just want to be loved.

Put your sunglasses on

Hey you,
put your sunglasses on and come with me,
we can dance under the stars and swim
in stranger´s pools,
we are young and we know
that nothing really matters than somebody
who
puts the sunglasses on
and follows wherever he wants to go,
so,
hey you, let's go.

I´m on my way

„Who are you?"

„I´m still on my way"

Collecting

still collecting
my world
while sitting
here
alone
sitting here
while waiting
for a sign

Painting my pain

sometimes my whole life is a pain,
everyday hurts and I ask myself how
I became like this,
and than I take the brush
and I take these colours and start
to paint,
painting my pain,
colour for colour,
ache for ache

Hurt somebody

we are so good in hurting,
like it is in our blood,
that sometimes we forget
that all we want is being safe

- it´s not our intention to leave wounds,
but we do it anyway

Memory

The memory of us is like the last sentence of a good
story,
it´s beautiful and leaves you enchanted,
but you also know it´s over and that makes you feel
sad and melancholic too.

The worth of my life

Sometimes I imagine that you die, from one day to
another.
That I loose everything, my whole world, the whole
universe.
That there would nothing stay as silence.
And than I realize
that not we are the ones who create the worth of our life,
it´s the people around us,
the ones,
who
determine
about
who we are.

Love Letter

I found those old love letters to you
and from one moment to the other,
all the feelings,
all the memories,
all the words
were back
and I realized that those feelings
will never leave,
they just fade away,
day by day
a little more.

Bravest girl on earth

I am the bravest girl on earth
when I am with you

It will be better

It bleeds
but it will be better
because
there is something in us
which will always heal

Twelve years

With the age of twelve I started writing
because I hated reading
I wasn´t interesting in words and literature
so I created something on my own
and than
my life began to be a system
of words and poetry

Tough

Isn´t it strange
that the thought of being with you is as tough
as the thought of being without you?

And so we were,
always a little bit like ice and fire,
like light and dark,
everything
and
nothing.

I don´t know

sometimes I don´t know how to behave
because I often got the feeling
that whatever I do
it´s always wrong

This morning

this morning I woke up
and for the first time after you came into my life
I wished somebody beside me
who isn´t you
somebody who smiles at me in the morning
gives me safeness
who isn´t you
so now I know
I´m back
and I´m not afraid anymore
that love can still come into my life
new sweet love

Can´t help me anymore

my head
my heart
my body
everything
seems to be so far away
and my soul
and my thoughts
seem to be strangers,
so these are the moments
I cant help me anymore
with anything,
because I lie when I say
it will be everything fine
because it is always
so far away from fine

- so I just start to wait for a wonder

It´s me

you crossed my way today
in the supermarket
you saw me with the messy hair
and tired eyes
and your eyes developed to big balls
like you forgot
that i exist
or you just expected me not like that
but hey,
it´s me, baby,
it´s me who runs through the floors
like a ghost in a cage

Today

Today
I am not afraid
I am not afraid
of
everything

Lover, come over

can somebody please
ring on the door
and tell me
that I am beautiful
and embrace me
like
you came in my life,
so surprisingly,
so without warning
with so much love
to give

Timeline

sometimes I see my life
in a timeline
and there are those special days
in big letters,
the date marked,
because some days
will never fade

Begin Again

sometimes you just have to forget yesterday
sometimes looking back to the old days is a bad idea
because
sometimes
we just must
begin
to begin again

Dream

My dreams changed

yesterday
I wanted to save the world

today
I don´t know If I even want to go out of my bed

dreams change
but sometimes
the old ones will lead us our way

Every little tiny dot

I hope
one day we will all look
into the mirror
and love
every
little
tiny
dot
of us

- Give love to your body, give love to your soul

You are free

You are free.
There are demons inside your veins
and sometimes you feel like you are in a prison.
But look around you my dear,
you are safe,
you have nothing to loose,
you are free,
so don´t ever be afraid
of breathing.

Slave

last night
i could not sleep
because sometimes
i become a slave of my thoughts
loosing
every piece of my own

Ghost

you make me feel
melancholical
on this sunday afternoon
although you left months ago
but your ghost
is still here
always around my neck
at that place
you last touched

Too sensitive

They say it´s a blessing
to be so sensitive like I am.
But most of the time
I feel like someone throws
me through the world
without any protective armor.

Every step too loud,
smell too strong
word too hard,
love too less
makes me feel like shrinking
and that, believe me,
is no blessing.

Lost

some people think
young people are destroyed

but some people just even don´t know
that we are not broken

we are just
lost

Rain

sometimes the world
is full of rain
too cloudy to see clear

and than i wish that you come
and bring the summer back to me

Stay optimistic

I know it´s tough to stay optimistic after all those
torches and humiliations
I know it´s not easy to be strong anymore

But I know that one day you will look back
and see that optimism was the best thing you could
chose

So come on
and let the sun
shine again
on your skin

Without you

It needed some years
to understand how
small
how
nothing
how
lost
I would be
without the one
who is always there,
holding me the umbrella
on the rainy days
so
unconditionally
and
always

What would I do without you?

Mystery

„Love is a mystery“

„No. The people are the ones who make it so
inscrutable,
because *we* are all mysteries“

Enough

You cried enough.

Now it´s time
to stand up
and show the world you fear so much,
show yourself,
that now
your healing starts,
the part,
in which the broken girl
grows to a
gorgeous butterfly.

So set your wings

and

f l y.

Ultimately The Moon

You said you love
talking to the moon.
I recognized too late,
that *you* were the moon,
and that explained everything
because
in front of me
your mouth was always locked
and oh,
I was so blind,
I did not understand that you were the moon,
not the sun,
keeping your light inside you,
instead of looking if I´m warm enough,
always behaving so bright,
so perfectly unperfect,
tarned as the sun,
something that will never set,
but
you were the *moon*,
which also has his dark, covered sides,
and I
will not give up
searching for the real sun.

Thanks

Thanks to my first love
which gave me the inspiration for this poetry,
thanks for my demons which think they can destroy me
but at least give me the power for finding my own voice
in this,
thanks for the people I love
because they make my life such so
beautiful and bright
and are the reason why the world mostly
looks like a warm and bloomy place for me.

* * *

And now, dear you,
please do me a favor
and bloom
like your blossoms
never lost their colours.

Yours,
Greta